MEMORIES
Words over Time

VICTOR STRINGER

A publication of

Eber & Wein Publishing

Pennsylvania

Memories: Words over Time

Copyright © 2023 by Victor Stringer

All rights reserved under the International and Pan-American copyright conventions. No part of this book may be reproduced, stored in a retrieval system, or transmitted in any form, electronic, mechanical, or by other means, without written permission of the author.

Library of Congress
Cataloging in Publication Data

ISBN 978-1-60880-756-7

Proudly manufactured in the United States of America by

Eber & Wein Publishing
Pennsylvania

CONTENTS

A Young Warrior's Request! 1
Alone in the Dark 3
Another Day Part II 6
Anything Electric 7
A Pirate's Life for Me! 8
A Broken Heart 10
Butterflies 11
Dad, Come Out and Play! 12
Diminished Love 13
Caterpillar 14
The Puppy and the Flea 16
Black 17
Belonging to You 18
Being with You 19
Endless Delight 20
Fool in Love 21
Forsaken Love 22
Just a Wonderful Dream 23
I Am You; You Are Me 25
I Do 26
Intoxicating Voyage 27
Is Cupid Dead? 29
It's Time to Leave 30
Morning Walk on the Beach 31
No Poem 32
Prayer 33
Desert Floor 34

Yogi Time 36
Visiting Nun 38
Unfaithfulness 40
Your Eyes 42
Top of the Morn, My Love 43
Two Sides of a Broken Heart 44
Broken Seashells 45
Thomas Miller 46
The Retreat 47
Thee 49
The Great Wars of 280 and 279 BC 50
The Coyote 51
Surrender 53
The Attic 54
Stuff 55
Silent Walk 56
Quiet Whisper 58
Poets Never Die 59
Poet's Frustration 60
Our Time Together Is Slipping Away 62
Old Blue Notebooks 64
Peace of Mind 66
6/22/2010 66
My Town 67
Metamorphous 70
My Love for You 71
Luxembourg 72
Love: A Question 73
Love Is Love 74

A Young Warrior's Request!

You call your young men and women to war.
I answer by lining up to volunteer and fight
while you, Mr. Politician, stay at home and play your silly,
never-ending political games.
If not blind to the real world, you refuse to see,
it is not dying that bothers me—
it is living without liberty!
If you politicians have your way
all our liberties will be voted away!
People in other countries live under dictatorships and ternary.
Who else but the US and our allies
can help set all these worthy people free?
Mr. Congressman (woman) you called me to fight,
to take down this tyrant with all of America's might.
Now it's time for you to seek re-election and you choose
to forget your words that put us here in the middle of this war,
the war you now say you don't support anymore!
You no longer see a world in pain;
all you see is your own personal gain.
I'm just a young warrior here on the battlefield,
praying I will be able to survive until my next meal.
I would not presume to tell you what to do.
I can only suggest you search your heart;
I pray the answers will come to you!
I ask myself do you really care how my friends and I feel,
or are you more concerned about your next political deal?
People at home protest this war because of your lies.
They protest as if they have nothing better to do.
We are here fighting and dying to keep our homeland free!
Why can't they see, their mindless protests
cause so much pain for my fellow fighters and me?

You voted to send us here to "fight the great fight,"
so you could go home and sleep safe at night!
Why did you vote for this war if
you were unsure it was the right thing to do?
Because that is exactly what it appears you have done.
What if because of your lies, we had all thrown down
our weapons and said, "We are through!
We don't like this war—we are not going to fight anymore!"
Because that is exactly what it appears you have done!

2016

Alone in the Dark

Here I sit alone in the dark
Somewhere in the distance
I hear a dog bark

The hour is late
For some reason I find
Myself concerned about my fate

Though I am sitting alone
Everyone important
Is here at home

They are all asleep
With pillows under their heads
And covers over their feet

Warm on a cold night
Nothing too disturbed
Nothing to create a fright

My day has been very long
I am tired, weary
Unable to sleep

All of my problems seem
To be piled in a very large
Mental heap

I know there is really nothing
That can't wait until tomorrow
Why then am I filled with such sorrow?

All this thinking won't make things right
Worrying just makes
For a very long night

I close my eyes in an attempt
To shut out the moonlight
Hoping to sleep through the night

I count to ten wishing to sleep
I even find myself
Trying to count sheep

My mind is racing
What to do, how do I
Stop all this pacing?

I am not solving any
Of these problems, they all remain
Locked in this mental game

A thought comes to mind
This is all too much for me
Sleep alone will set me free

Out of the night a voice comes
So loud you see, almost as if
Someone was standing next to me!

This voice I have heard before
Perhaps, last night, perhaps
The night before

You know that I am here
I can help you, this you know
Have no fear

Put all your trouble
In a big brown bag up on the shelf
Marked "Let go and let God!"

I fall deep in sleep
Awake in the morning
Rested and at peace!

2008

Another Day Part II

The last time I saw you in this park,
I turned and ran away.
Apprehensive, unable to express my feeling,
I had difficulty getting to sleep that night . . .
or any other night since.
I returned today
because I can no longer live
thinking about you this way!
I must find a way to express how I feel.
I'm running about as if I were on a Ferris wheel;
I see you across the park once again!
All my emotions are grinding inside of me;
I feel as if I'm about to commit an angry sin!
All at once you start walking towards me.
You appear to be looking directly at me!
I am unable to move, hypnotized by what I see.
You walk as if you are a runway model—
hair black as midnight,
skin the color of extra virgin olive oil,
legs that go on forever
as they connect to your long, lean body,
eyes black as new dug coal.
Your smile could set the sun on fire.
You are more beautiful to me than
Monet's "Woman in the Garden" in springtime.
Everyone in the park seems to pause and gaze when you pass.
The warm afternoon breeze flirts with your hair.
Powerless to stand it any longer, I turn again to run away.
When I hear you say, "Didn't I see you here the other day?"
I turn to see if you are speaking to me.
You walk up, hold out your hand to me and say . . .
Just then the clock alarm went off.
I awoke as my image of you faded away!

Anything Electric

While traveling to
San Diego
I tell my young daughter
we will have to cross the
Coronado Bridge
She says I don't like bridges
or airplanes
I ask her why
She says Dad
I don't like planes or bridges
Planes and bridges could crash
then we could be killed
I say look at it this way
If the bridge were to fall or
the plane were to crash
we would go to Heaven
together
and get our wings
We would be together
forever
She says Dad I don't
want to go to Heaven
I am only seven
I don't even have a
cell phone, an iPad
a computer
or
anything electric

A Pirate's Life for Me!

To all the young men who grew up wanting to be a pirate!

The captain sailed his forty guns, four masts ship, its holes overfilled with the booty from his most recent raid, from the dock and headed full sail out to sea. In his cabin, chained, a captive chambermaid.

It was time to leave this ravaged port for the open sea to seek a safer haven elsewhere for his ship and crew. This port was no longer a place he desired to be! The tide was right; he sensed a strong storm about to brew.

Thunderous seas tossed his mighty ship to and fro. Having sailed these stormy waters in the past, he knew to head the ship towards the moonlight's glow. As an experienced sailor he knew well this storm would not last.

At last, the vessel was freed from the island's coast. With a man in the crow's nest, a few men on the sails, the master had another victory of which he would boast! He laughed as he watched crew members throwing up over the rails!

As he navigated his ship, its black sails sucking up the sea breeze, his most important task now was to keep his ship upright. This was the kind of night that would bring normal men to their knees, praying they would survive this infernal night!

The ship was now making great time, though it was still being tossed about by the harshness of the sea. The winds seemed to be settling, which helped ease the captain's mind. He knew that soon this great wind would become just a breeze.

Above the main sail, its skull and cross bones, flag flying high for all to see! Since he was a young lad, this ship had been his home. For this master, there was no other place he preferred to be.

All the years of fighting had left him scarred from head to toe. There was little doubt he was growing older every day. His once jet black beard was now as white as windblown snow!

He often questioned himself, "How much longer can I live this way?"

A Broken Heart

Yesterday we spoke of love
We seemed blessed from above
We kissed we hugged

Bonding our undying love
Today I awoke at dawn
To find you gone

I am perplexed
As you must know
Wondering, why you had to go

We spoke of a future together
You must have thought of us apart
Now I am alone, a broken heart

2011

Butterflies

We all have them
They come into
Our lives as if
From nowhere and
Bring joy for the moment

They are all very
Lovely in their own
Ways. They exist
In many varieties
Colors, sizes, shapes

One thing they all
Have in common
Their frivolousness
Interested mostly in
Their own trivial pleasures

Try as you might
To seek some form
Of contact, they fly
Away returning
To their own world

Leaving you alone
Desiring their return
To share that pleasure
You know is fleeting
Yet needed from time to time

9/14/2010

Dad, Come Out and Play!

Goodnight, my sweet princess,
I can tell you're tired from your big yawn.
It is dark outside; this day is gone!
The castle lights are going out
so you can sleep and dream of tomorrow's dawn.
You awoke this morning at the break of day;
you have spent the day with your friends at play.
You ran on the beach and made castles of sand;
you played hide and seek with your friends.
Each time you got caught, you laughed and ran.
When you say, "Dad, come out and play,"
your smile always makes my day!
I try to keep up with you the best I can,
but all I feel is that I am becoming an old man!
Each day you fill me with so much joy and love;
I know in my heart you are a gift from our Lord above!
I am tired myself and want to go to sleep;
however, I will give you a piggyback ride to show my love.
Then I'll tell you the stories of Little Bow Peep,
Goldie Locks and The Three Bears,
after which I want you to say your prayers.
Then I will hug you hard and kiss your cheeks,
for each time I do so, my heart skips a beat.

2009

Diminished Love

Ego
Clouds
Create
Shadows
Of
Despair
Genesis
Unfaithful
Lover
Crushing
All
Emotion
Creating
Distrust
In
All
Other
Parts
Of
One's
Being

6/8/2010

Caterpillar

A young boy walking in the park one day
sees a green caterpillar on a branch
high up in a large willow tree.
He thinks, that caterpillar appears
to be looking at me.
The boy hears the caterpillar say,
"What are you doing in the park
so far from home?"
The boy replies, "I was out walking
and lost my way."
The caterpillar says, "That has happened
to me before.
Maybe fifty times or more!"
The boy asks, "What should I do?"
The caterpillar says, "I can tell you are sad.
You must be missing your mom and dad.
It's such a great day;
perhaps you can stay a while.
You and I can find a game to play—
something to make you smile."
They play for much of the day.
The caterpillar crawls up and down
the boy's arms and tickles his hands.
It's difficult to believe a
boy and a caterpillar could have so much fun.
The boy falls asleep.
When he awakes, the caterpillar is gone.
He looks up into the tree and all he sees
is a large brown cocoon hanging
from a branch.
The boy leaves the park

and finds his way back home.
He feels sad . . . he lost his friend that day.
He wonders if it was all a dream.
The next day he returns to the park
hoping to find his friend,
hoping they might play.
He arrives just in time to see
the large cocoon open
and a beautiful yellow and blue butterfly
fly away.
The boy is sure he heard
the butterfly say,
"Thanks for being my friend.
Make it a great day."

2/16/2009

The Puppy and the Flea

A little brown and white puppy
likes to play around a large white birch tree
in front of its house.
The puppy's best friend was a tiny flea.
Everywhere the puppy went
the tiny flea would be,
jumping up and down on the puppy's back,
tickling and chasing it around
that large birch tree.
One day the puppy brought the flea home
to meet its family.
The puppy told its dad, "I have a new friend;
I want it to live with me."
The puppy's father's fur became very itchy.
He told the puppy, "This cannot be—
that flea must go."
The puppy cried "No, no, no!
I love the flea, and it loves me!"
The dad said, "I know you love that flea;
however, it is different, not like us you see.
We are dogs and we really can't
live with fleas."

2/16/2009

Black

Black as night
Black hole
Black crayon
Black knight
Black bark
Black on black
Black bird
Black balled
Black ace
Black light
Black stone
Black oak
Black rose
Black eye
Fade to black

August 2010

Belonging to You

I want to belong to you
As the ocean belongs to the horizon
Stars to the sky
Rain to the clouds

I want to belong to you
As darkness belongs to the night
Sun to the daytime
Thunder to lightning

I want to belong to you
As nighttime becomes daytime
One and one make two
Flame of a candle

I want to belong to you
As the child belongs to the mother
Stream to the river
Fish to the sea

I want to belong to you
As sand to the beach
Peanut butter to jelly
Coffee to cream

I want to belong to you
As no one ever has
Life to death
I want to belong to you!

October 2010

Being with You

Being with you
Is like a walk on any
Beach on a Sunday afternoon
The first break of sunrise
Breakfast at Tiffany
Sitting on a park bench
Holding hands in Central Park
Lunching at Tavern on the Green
Dining atop the Eifel Tower
Watching the changing
Of the guard at Buckingham Palace
Being the first astronaut on the moon
Playing nude in the water
At paradise beach on the
Island of Mikonos, Greece
Watching the storms over Cuba
Like a great fireworks display
From a sandy beach at sunset
On Montego Bay, Jamaica
"No problem man"
Sharing the first puppy love kiss
Holding hands in a foreign film
With subtitles not caring
About the plot
Every moment a new beginning
Each touching a new sensation
Each sensation a new awakening
Of love to long unknown
Needing a lifetime to experience

9/10/2010

Endless Delight

As you lay next to me in the dark
I can feel the quick beating of my heart
This is the first night we have stayed together
My breath is floating above us, light as a feather

My mind is filled with desire and delight
Since we met I have dreamed of this night!
My body is somewhere between being on fire and
Preparing for flight, yet I know that being here is right!

I sense your body shiver
Or is it me trembling in ecstasy?
All at once I feel your hands move over me
Now I surrender to your loving embrace

My trembling hands wonder the beauty
Can it be that my dreams have at last come true?
My body is on fire as our arms entwine
I pull you closer as I sense it is time

As I enter slowly your world of endless delight
I know in my heart it was important
We waited to share this moment of our love
On this our wedding night!

2009

Fool in Love

Shadows have fallen over my chosen path
as I remember the words you spoke last.
I can't seem to recall you ever having spoken
to me like this in the past.
Your words came as such a surprise;
they were so harsh I couldn't
keep the tears from swelling up in my eyes.
I tried to close my ears,
not wanting to hear the words I feared.
Everyone told me this day would come
when you would pack up and run!
I kept saying she loves me too much to stray.
When you came home and said you were leaving me
I realize now what a fool I was to think
our love could end in any other way!
I am ashamed to admit that to anyone
other than myself that I was a fool in love.

2009

Forsaken Love

I thought I knew you really well;
we have been together for so long.
How could I have been so wrong?
All those days and nights we shared—
you acted as if you really cared.
All along someone else lived
in the shadows of our relationship.
You said you knew him before I came along.
You loved him; however, he loved another.
You refused to accept his pleas,
"Just let me be, live your life, and set me free."
I have given you all my love.
I can no longer live with my head in the sand;
my heart is broken beyond repair.
I can no longer live with the ghost of another man;
there is nothing left of me to share.
Since you love this other person so,
there is nothing left for me but to let you go.
I leave with but one regret—
I did not know of your forsaken love when we met.
All the love I have shared with you
that could have never been.
Truly we both lost in the end.

2007

Just a Wonderful Dream

My family and I went to the circus today.
There were big gray elephants, yellow tigers,
brown and black bears, and large camels for all to see.
We saw some monkeys swinging in a tree.
The parade of buses and cars filled with clowns drove by.
We saw birds of yellow, blue, green, and white flying up high.
There was even a clown dressed like a baby,
sucking on a very large bottle, pretending to cry!
This was not my first time at a circus;
I had been to the circus before
when I was two or three, or was I four?
I did not remember that a circus could be so much fun.
Mom, Dad, and I laughed out loud when we saw a horse
being ridden by a cowboy clown!
Two other clowns rode on two horses' butts.
We ate cotton candy, popcorn, peanuts,
and drank Cokes until we could eat or drink no more;
my mom said we would all get sick for sure.
The ring master blew his whistle, and the show began.
It started with a magic man with a big black hat on his hand.
He pulled out a white rabbit and then some white doves flew out;
I could not help it—I was so excited I had to shout!
Then came a man and woman dressed in red, white, and blue
outfits followed by at least twenty dogs;
I am sure none of them would ever bite.
After all the dogs had performed, they all ran through a white fog.
The whistle blew again, and girls all dressed up in very pretty dresses
rode out on a white horse. The girls jumped from one horse to another.
They did hand stands and ran alongside the horses and jumped on.
These were some of the greatest tricks I had ever seen.

I heard, "It's time to go." It was the voice of my mother. This was one of the best days of my life. I awoke and realized this had all been just a wonderful dream.

2008

I Am You; You Are Me

Out of darkness
I have come
For I have discovered, you see
I am you; you are me!

Into the light
Is where I wish to go
Now that I see
I am you; you are me!

For the future, I go
Within me an internal glow
For now I know, you see
I am you; you are me.

We will travel throughout eternity
You and me:
Now I can reach for infinity.
I am you; you are me.

My heart is full
As it can be
Now that I know, you see
I am you; you are me.

From this earth I'm set free
Walking the path to infinity.
There is no other place for me to be.
I am you; you are me.

I am healthy, happy, and holy.
How else could I be
Since I have discovered
I am you; you are me!

I Do

True love is difficult to find
Many frogs get kissed along the way
The search can vex the mind
Some loves stay for years
Some for just a day!
Many lovers may come and go
Some remain friends, others become foes
How then is a person supposed to know?
When all this endless searching is through
There is one thing for sure "there is no sure thing"
One never knows what the next romance will bring
Perhaps, a lot of pain
Or, best of all, the church bells will ring!
I, for one, should never give love advice
However, I would suggest you be very careful
When you choose that princess to be your wife
Make sure you know in your heart she is the one
You wish to be with for the rest of your life
Be very sure that all your seed sowing is through
Before you give away your heart and say "I do"

2002

Intoxicating Voyage

Lavender sky brings to life
The early morning light
Last night's full lucent moon
Floats high in the westerly sky
Illuminated by the eastward rising sun
Half a dozen black pelicans drift
Over the slow-moving ocean waves
As they float like a disciplined corps
Headed south toward Mexico
The thunder of the surf echoes
Along the damp gray sandy beach as it
Slams onto the shore once more
Before riding the receding tide
Towards the eastern horizon
Never to return to this
Deserted sandy oasis
Seashells are abandoned by
Their sea faring inhabitants as they
Acquire new armor to protect
Them for a continuing growth cycle on the
Bottom of the Pacific Ocean's floor
A lone white sail appears out of the south
Headed north along the shimmering coast
Towards some unknown destination
As I sit here drinking my first cup of creamed coffee
Thinking about you, I seem to move
Slowly towards an uncharted destination
My sails are unfurled, searching for soft trade winds
To guide me into calm warm waters of a secure harbor
Lying in your tender, loving, desiring arms

Last night engendered in me a wanton desire
To press forward through the impending squall
Trusting my internal emotional compass
To steer my audacity forward on
This magnificent intoxicating voyage

2010

Is Cupid Dead?

Fifteen years of a loving relationship
Destroyed by an affair (via Facebook)
That broke our family apart
Sleepless nights follow
Days of endless unanswerable questions
As to what I might have done to foresee
These mindless destructive events
Blindness—yes that is the answer!
Willful blindness to past betrayal
Past betrayal which should have been
A sign post of things to come
Life now is covered by dark clouds
Of uncertainty hovering over my daily life
Is this the beginning or the ending
Or something great? Is Cupid dead?
You call me and say you are sorry (for what)
I really don't know what you are doing!
Are you seeking answers to your problems from me?
You say your life is shattered, it is like
You are unaware that you are the one who
Slipped away from our family with all your phone calls
And endless emails to your "friends"
I have no answers, only unanswerable questions

October 2010

It's Time to Leave

I gave you
My time
My heart
My love
You say
I want to leave
There's nothing
Left to do
Except admit
We are through
Now there is one
Where once
There were two

2009

Morning Walk on the Beach

As I walk on the beach at sun up
the sky is bright with large white clouds appearing to be taking flight
The waves a chasing on the beach, the water is ice cold as it washes up
over my bear feet
As I walk alone my thoughts are of you, sitting alone at home
Black and white seagulls land on the beach
each appearing to be looking for something to eat
I see a large brown dog sniffing the sand
running from spot to spot chasing the aroma of himself or another
Seashells everywhere having been deposited on the beach
before the ocean waters could retreat
Looking up at the cliffs arising from the earth
as if that had exploded from some ancient violent birth
The sunlight plays tricks with the morning dew
The dark showers hide much of the cliff's beauty from my view
White clouds flow in the sky so blue
My thoughts return again to you—how I wish you were here
to enjoy this splendid view
Many a morning we walked this beach together
What happened between you and me?
Why did you have to say goodbye?
I see a couple walking barefoot in the sand
As they pass me walking hand in hand
I see in their eyes a love I once knew
when I used to take this walk with you
No longer can I hold your hand
as we walk along the sand
God has called you to come play on His heavenly beach

2/20/2009

No Poem

I did not
write a poem
today

I could not
think of a
thing to say

As I recall
there was no poem
yesterday

I guess we
will just have
to wait and see

Perhaps I will
not write a poem
tomorrow

August 25, 2010

Prayer

There must be a place
Where I may see God's face
Where love is shown each day
Where I can serve God in every way
Let me find that place
Where I may see God's face
No words need to be spoken
No tears need to be shed
Where God's love surrounds me
Where God's love will set me free
Show me the place of God's face
Where all I see and feel
Will be a reflection of God's grace
Where no words are needed to experience
All the love of God's grace
I will surrender all to God in this place
So please lead me to this place
Where I may see God's face

May 21, 2010

Desert Floor

Here we sit, my fellow marines and me
on this hot Dhi-Oar desert floor
surrounded by the effects of this maddening war.
I am a marine who came to Iraq to fight for liberty—
not just for the people of my country.
We came here to help these people to be free.
Some people at home march in the streets
in protest of this war
as they have during other wars.
They carry banners and shout, "War no more!
Who needs this war?"
They claim we should leave this country
and bring our warriors home—
so much anger!
The politicians who voted for the war
now are questioning why we are still here,
why more of our young people have to die.
It is true many have died in this war
as have many died before.
This is a sacrifice we make for liberty,
for we live in a country that is free
while these people live under a dictatorship and tyranny.
Perhaps, it is time for our countrymen and politicians
to stop sending mixed messages
that give aid and comfort to our enemies.
We need to show a united front in this fight;
then the world and our enemies will know we are right
to help these people in their fight for liberty.
Many local warriors fight at our side so they, too, can be free.
There is still much work to be done;

this is not the time to "cut and run."
Each of us knows what it is to be free.
That's what war should be about
for my fellow warriors and me!

2002

Yogi Time

Deep in a forest high on a hill,
I sat on a rock becoming very still
in a yogi crossed-legged lotus position.
Finding peace from within was my mission
as I concentrated on my breathing—
breathing out to release my negative emotion,
breathing in to enjoy all that lie before me.
I just wanted to release my being over to my senses,
trying to let go all my superfluous defenses.
My yogi once said, "Meditation should not be used
in order to accept one's self; the purpose should be to become more
aware of one's place in the universe."
As I relaxed, I was overcome with the smells and sounds
of nature's never-ending splendor around me!
I could hear baby birds chirping in a tree near me.
Off in the distance, the sound of a coyote's cry.
Overhead a gaggle of gray geese flew by.
I felt the cool spray of the waterfall just behind me.
The smell of honeysuckles filled the calm air.
I was no longer conscious of night or day.
What did it matter anyway? I was on my way!
Back to where I have been many times before
as I descended further into myself.
I felt as if I were a cloud flowing high in the sky.
Yielding to the moment, prepared to just let things be,
a great wave of emotion flooded my being!
I was aware of a spiritual presence enveloping me!
Chills ran from my head down to my feet and back again!
A bright golden light seemed to cover me from head to toe.
I knew in my heart I had arrived; there was nowhere to go!
A peace seemed to take control.

All my fears were left behind. My eyes seemed to open
as never before—where I had been blind, now I could see!
From all my illusions vanished my spirit was set free.
In this moment of awareness, I knew I could never
return to the life I had known.
After all, God had allowed me to sit down near His thrown.
His hand touched the top of my head as He said, "You have
lots of work left to be done. When it is complete I will
bring you back home. I will remain in your heart and
will be there whenever you need me.
You are never alone!
I live in your heart, which is My home!"
As I awoke from my meditation, I had the feeling
I was not alone. I knew I would come here
again as I had so many times before.
I know, God, that each time I do,
I will grow stronger in spirit and mind.
I will move closer with You!

2005

Visiting Nun

Pneumonia
Engulfed
My 17 years
Young body
Hospitalized
Lungs enflamed
Filled to capacity
Mucus running
Up my station
Tubes
Tear drops forming
On the ear
Drums exploding ripping
The membrane
Beyond repair
Temperature 104 degrees
In a coma
Over two weeks
Lost 48 pounds
Virus omitting
From my lungs
Infected members
Of the hospital's staff
During one night
Of excruciating agony
There appeared at
My bedside
A fully habited
Velvety speaking nun
The room filled
With her presence

She touched my
Arm offering me
Life from a
Glass of orange juice
The following morning
Hearing my story
My doctor said
There has never
Been any nuns
At this hospital
I know she
Was there or
I would not
Be here at
Age 68
Years young

June 30, 2010

Unfaithfulness

I sit here painfully alone
Witness to a shattered world
Turned upside down

Unfaithfulness
My heart irreparably broken
The sea of tears have yet not subsided
The eternal sleepless nights abound

Unfaithfulness
Where do I go from here
Any attempt to reconcile
Seems only to widen the abyss

Unfaithfulness
There do not appear to be any solutions
Only a myriad of unanswerable questions
The tormenting pain consumes my being

Unfaithfulness
Days and nights cruelly merge
Lost hours become lost days
Memories become haunting nightmares

Unfaithfulness
Expectations of a solidarity future
Drown in a pool of poignant tears
Of one despondently left behind

Unfaithfulness
The two have become a deserted one
Abandoned in the darkness of despair
Sitting deserted I wonder why

Unfaithfulness

Your Eyes

When I look into your eyes
I see the light of my soul,
the reflections of lives past,
the doorway to the future.

When I look into your eyes
I see the sun on a cloudy day,
the moon shining
on a dark and dreary night.

When I look into your eyes
I see the calm and peace
at knowing your eyes have
found what they were seeking.

When I look into your eyes
I see you looking from within
and calling to me, allowing
me to know of your love.

When I look into your eyes
I see myself looking into my
own eyes, seeing the person
I have been searching for.

When I look into your eyes
I see that now I can enjoy
being at peace with one person,
having completed my journey!

Top of the Morn, My Love

Come rest in the heather
with me and let desires
direct our time together

Let the morning sun warm our
naked bodies and light a
fire in our loving hearts

Each kiss brings another spark
building the fire within us
until our passion is our only purpose

Let our love and passion
move us through the daylight until
the moon shines upon our repose

Two Sides of a Broken Heart

We used to walk this beach late at night,
walking hand in hand in the moon's bright yellow light,
hovering over the ocean, holding the night's darkness at bay.
As it lit up the beach and guided our way,
we strolled near the water's edge.
The calm waves washed the imprints of our footsteps away,
leaving the beach as clean as if we were never there.
I remember each of our walks as if they were yesterday.
Each time I return to this place I am reminded of
how the moonlight would glow on your face.
Your dark eyes and your long black hair would shine.
I am reminded of the night you gave me
one side of a broken heart,
a symbol you said, "that we would never part."
Since you left me, I find myself walking this beach
alone from time to time,
reading your letter over and over.
You said you were sorry things had to end this way.
What brings tears to my eyes
more than the words of your letter is your half
of the broken heart taped to the bottom of the page.
I have no doubt in my mind and heart
you will never return.
As much as I love you,
I have felt you would leave me from the start.
This, however, does not ease the pain I feel
as I stand here on the sand holding both sides of this broken
heart.

2009

Broken Seashells

Broken seashells on the shore
Where we used to walk
Where we used to talk
Things we don't do anymore

The surf hugs the white sandy shore
Warm breezes blow over the beach
Flooding my memories of
Things we don't do anymore

Single footprints mark the sand
Where two used to be
Now only me, thinking about
Things we don't do anymore

Standing alone tears fill my eyes
As the sun descends towards the horizon
Darkness enfolds the night sky, I ponder
Things we don't do anymore

Thomas Miller

Thomas Miller and I were friends
We swore we would be until the end
We were playmates for as long
As anyone could remember
We shared our life together that is until
The month of September
The year was 1964
When my friend Thomas Miller
Went off to the Vietnam War
Thomas Miller wrote home almost every day
Seems he has a great deal to say
His letters were filled with stories
About this strange faraway war
Thomas Miller like many others who
Attended this foreign campaign
Could not understand why
They were there
One day Thomas Miller's
Letters stopped coming
The last letter came from
The War Department
It read, "We are sorry to report
Thomas Miller died today
In the Vietnam War"
The month of October
The year was 1964

2010

The Retreat

In the early
morning dew
I park the car
at the top of the hill.
I descend
into the valley
down a long white
staircase covered in
ivy vines
crowned with
small white flowers.

Fragrance of honeysuckles
drifts on the warm breeze.
At the bottom of the stairs
is a dirt path
bordered with
white and red
roses
violets
lavender
enjoyed by bees and butterflies
celebrating the way.

Across a wooden bridge
over a babbling brook
near the cottage
with blue shutters
surrounded by a white
picket fence

a straw mat
lay in front
of the red door
with words
My Retreat.

August 2010

Thee

Red apples
Golden pears
Eating purple orchids
Red-white wine
Silent walks
Sunsets
Indigo sky
Sunrise
Afternoon rendezvous
Sleepless nights
Late night talks
Morning coffee
Writing poems
Sharing poems
Donne
Miller
Lawrence
Whitman
Things that
Remind me
Of thee

2010

The Great Wars of 280 and 279 BC

King Pyrrhic slashes through ancient lands,
far from the kingdom he called home.
Many a battle he fought, hand to hand,
against the battle-hardened warriors of Rome.

As a great king he knew the cost to his men.
Their wives, loved ones, and family he left behind.
For this king the human loss was a great sin,
which weighed heavy on his mind.

There were the great wars of 280 and 279 B.C.
Pyrrhic's armies were well-trained and able to carry the
fight. To their enemies, both on land an at sea,
the victories seemed hollow and troubled the king each night!

Both armies fought bravely and lost many men.
The Roman leaders appeared amoral to those lost.
Pyrrhic worried—were the victories worth it in the end?
He prayed nightly to be forgiven for this mortal cost.

His army fought by day, buried their men by night.
He was even forced to bury his best friend.
So many battles won, but were the losses worth the fight?
Would his broken heart be able to survive to the war's end?

No quarter ask, no quarter was anyone giving.
Though he has lost many of his fine warriors in this fight,
his fight now was for the brave men living.
He knew many fine souls would enter Heaven's gates tonight!

January 11, 2006

The Coyote

I visited a local
Indian burial site today
My second visit
I had heard about
The site for many years

On my first visit
The four markers were
In need of repair
I stood up three of the
Markers and replaced seashells

A coyote
Was running along
A nearby wire fence
He appears to be
Looking me over

It is so rare to see
A coyote during daylight
I remember seeing
One many years ago
In the California desert

Hundreds of crows were flying
Over the burial site
What a strange phenomenon
I experienced an eerie feeling
As if great spirits were there

It was as if the coyote
And the black birds
Were in some way
Protecting the fallen
Residing at this site

Several weeks later
I returned to the site
It was the middle of the day
The coyote was still there
Protecting this sacred site

9/14/2010

Surrender

Come rest in the silence
of my loving arms.
Let the night ease away
from us like a floating cloud
in the evening sky.

Let the worries of the day
leave your mind and body.
Surrender to the moment and
let your thoughts mingle
with the pleasure you desire.

In the silence our minds and bodies
will blend with our passion,
two hearts beating as one,
each giving to the other
unbound passion and love.

The Attic

Boxes
Trunks
Doll house
Stuffed toys
Old clothing and shoes
Rocking chair
Bowling balls
Stakes
Barbie dolls
Photo albums
Lettermen jackets
Wedding dress
Military uniform
Slingshot
Snow skies
Tax records

Stuff

Broken baby carriage
Animal carry box
Part of retreated truck tire
Extension ladder
Lawn rake
Weekend ice chest
Red tennis shoes
Tennis rackets
Clothing
Mile-long streak of toilet paper
Broken kitchen cabinet
Black tool chest
Yellow couch
Bike tire and rim
Black and red bicycle
California highways

Silent Walk

I want to remember a silent walk with you
Not speaking to each other at all
Not having to fill the time with words
Just enjoying the moments together

Feeling the warm wind as it passes us by
Hearing a bird song as it floats on the evening breeze
Experiencing the sounds of the waves rushing onto the shore
Then seeing them washing back to the open ocean

Feeling the tepid white sand beneath our feet
Seeing the footprints of others who have
Adventured here before us
Wondering who they were, where they might be going

Were they talking with each other
What past they might be sharing
Or were they, too, just content exploring together
While on a silent walk, just enjoying the moments

I want to remember feeling the afternoon heat from the setting sun
Upon our faces as we marveled at the reflection of
The sun's fiery flow floating upon the ocean's waves
As it disappeared across the distant horizon

As we return to the place we have just come from
A cool breeze touches our backs
Was it the chill I experience from the night breeze
Or was it the feeling I enjoyed of you being at my side

We are no longer the people who walked up that beach
We experienced each other in a very special way
Not talking or touching, just feeling our hearts beat
Closing the void that two people feel many moments in their lives

There was no need to speak or touch
The unspoken words were felt between us
No words could express the joy we shared
As we took this silent walk into the future together

Quiet Whisper

You said
I love you
My heart skipped a beat
Tears filled my eyes
I was unable to speak
Your words
Floated on the air
Like a warm
Summer's mist
Landing on my
Bare chest
My breath slowed
To a quiet whisper

2012

Poets Never Die

The poet born in love
Travels the world
Through their thoughts
Translated into words
Which arise from their soul?
Speaking through the heart
Some words are sad others gay
Readers are transported by their words
In different ways
It is words the poet
Employs to share their
Views of the world
The use of metaphor
Is their palette, overflowing with
Flowers
Sunrises
Sunsets descending behind mountains
Waterfalls tumbling into
Streams, becoming rivers, rivers
Flowing into oceans
Valleys covered in yellow sunflowers
Moon's light illuminating distant horizons
The majesty of love
Heartbreak of betrayal
Long walks on deserted beaches
Life
Death
The reward of the poet's embrace
Of the world is their immortality
Poets never die

July 11, 2010

Poet's Frustration

Here I am, pen in hand
on a very hot sunny summer's day,
sitting under the cooling breeze
of a large five-bladed fan!
Blankness covers the pages
of this yellow-lined pad of paper
on this old oak desk in front of me.
Crumbled paper of imprecise words
discarded all over the workroom floor,
this is not the first time.
I have been here many times before.
It seems I have lost my facility
to write the verse of another poem.
I've been laboring here most of the day;
seems I've lost my poetic way!
So many times I have attempted to
give rise to the heart of a new rhythm.
Is it just another big waste of time?
Occasionally when I write the words flow
like the cool waters of a beautiful mountain stream.
At other times they come slowly
like an overloaded train on an uphill trek
running out of stream!
I am always looking for a new rhythm or a verse.
Or should I say that in reverse?
Should I write about a walk on the beach?
Perhaps, a trip to the mountains covered in snow!
A new love or an old love abandoned.
My mind is so fogged I truly don't know.
I have heard it said, "Writing is an art"—
then the words should come from the heart.

At present I feel like a lover who has lost their mate
or a painter who has misplaced a brush.
I am at a loss for words to express this feeling of loss.
I have spoken with other poets who have said,
"I know what you mean, I've been there.
It's sometimes so frustrating, you just want
to pull out your hair!"
Oh well, it's a bright sunny day out.
I'll just lay down my yellow-lined paper pad and pen
to return later and start all over again!

2009
revised 2010

Our Time Together Is Slipping Away

We sit at the side of the pool
Drinking beers and eating
Pasta and popcorn shrimp
Chimes ring overhead as
The cool afternoon breeze sticks the bells
It's as if the chimes are saying
Goodnight to the setting sun
Our time together is slipping away

We are committed to others
Loved ones who need us
We need them as well
My mind is screaming out to you
I want to say things to you
That no one has ever said to you before
I want you to know of my love
Our time is slipping away

I yearn to be the most important
Person in your life
I want to kiss your lips
In such a way that I touch your soul
To touch your body, to again experience
Your warmth exploding all over me
To hold you in my arms
Our time together is slipping away

We sit quietly knowing the time
Has come for us to again leave each other
To return to our other worlds
The worlds that refuse to release us
We hold each other, know that we
Will be together again soon
Not wanting to leave
Our time together is slipping away

We hug, we kiss our hearts are beating fast
I want to say things to you
I want you to know of my love for you
My thoughts fall into an abyss
The words are there, I just can't
Bring them to the surface
Is it too soon to share these feelings?
Our time together is slipping away!

2010

Old Blue Notebooks

I found several old blue notebooks today
of old poems at different stages of completion—
poems I had attempted writing many years ago.
I was amazed; I thought I had discarded these old books.

Why I wrote many of these words, I really don't know.
The notebooks were filled with many fragmentary poems,
many a scantily-written rhyme and verse—
some covered many pages,

some written only on one side of the page,
some crossed out and written on the opposite side,
incomplete poems of poorly-written expressions of love,
words of sadness, some spotted with tears of desires.

Poems with unfulfilled requests from Heaven above,
words meant to set one's lover's heart on fire,
poems to new loves, of loves lost,
poems started at the beach on a train on a plane.

Odes to life, love, to nothing at all—
as I read these words in progress I realized over the years
my life had changed; I had found a new voice,
one that expressed new feeling, desires, dreams.

These old works seem to be from a voice
I had not heard for several years.
I started to cry; I could not repress the stream of tears.
It seems I have lost much of my youthful passion for rhyme.

My heart was very heavy knowing
it is not always possible to bring
back one's youth of expression.
Life changes us all; that's the way of life.

I left these blue books of would-be poems
still unfinished
with a promise to re-examine them
should I ever heed that youthful voice again.

2/10/2009
Rev. 7/17/2010

Peace of Mind

As I sit meditating in the patio garden
warmed by the fading afternoon sun,
I am awakened by the fragrances
of roses, lilies, and violets, drifting
on the gentle passing breeze as it
brushes the bells of nearby chimes.
A robin, perched on the branch of a Japanese maple
tree, sings as if inspired by the music of the chimes.
A light mist from the waterfall cools my body.
I am aware of all that surrounds me;
however, it is in the silences between
all these pleasant distractions to my senses
where I find the peace that touches my soul.

6/22/2010

My Town

I live in a very
small town in the west.
In fact, it is so small
if you don't live here
it does not exist at all!

Our town is so small
we have to travel twenty miles
to visit a shopping mall!
We pack a lunch when we go that way;
the trip takes us all day.

The last time I went there by bus
I saw a fellow with a knapsack
on his back on the side of the road
carrying a cardboard sign that
read, "Somewhere else or bust!"

Main Street consists of a
hardware store, gas station-garage,
police station, a movie house, and
a Dairy Queen. On Saturday night
it's where everyone is seen.

We have only one policeman in town;
he has a difficult time getting around.
He is very old and can hardly see;
I can't remember the last time
he placed someone into custody.

Outside of farming, jobs are
few and far between.
Most of the young men
leave town before they are grown,
wanting badly to make it on their own.

Most leave because they don't
like working on the farms.
Now, when you drive around
you see "Help Wanted" signs
on many of the barns!

Our high school is a two-story
building located on
high on a tree-lined hill
right next to the old
closed lumber mill.

Our school football team
is known as the Wolf Pack.
The only time we ever
won a game, the coach got
so excited he died from a heart attack!

There are no virgins left in town.
There was one left, we were quite sure.
Then the circus came to play;
we are not truly sure anymore.
She left with the show, married to the clown!

I graduated with honors from our school.
I even went to church and learned
to live by the "Golden Rule!"
I still live and work in this town today.
I like it here—I can't imagine living any other way!

2009

Metamorphous

Living in the tragedy of the moment
The horrifying path between
The past and the future
The future having no meaning, it does not exist
The past has come to claim me
My arms outstretched, reaching for the dark
Clouding night's sky. Is this a prayer?
My hooved feet sinking deep into the blood
Covered ground beneath me
My wards no longer able to recognize me
Having turned against me, my transformation
Nearly complete, their canine bones breaking
Teeth and paws are ripping me apart
My accuser's bowstring has been drawn
Yet no arrow is dispatched to release me
From this penetrating and unbearable pain
Which I am obligated to endure as tribute
For my past indiscretions
I am no longer able to speak
My voice having long since departed
My mind is screaming!
Please, if you have any compassion
Release that arrow!

Poem inspired by a picture of the name.
By: Titan Circa 1500 AD.

2014

My Love for You

My love for you
Is as real as the sunrise
Moon's illuminating night skies
Light breeze on a summer's night
Rain on a sunny day
Dew on the morning roses
Thunder followed by lightning

My love for you
Is as real as the
Ocean's bathing
A white sandy beach
Rivers funneling into the oceans
The sutra's white sands
Morning red skies before a storm

My love for you
Is as real as
A newborn baby
Tears of joy
Shed by his mother
Love between
Romeo and Juliet

My love for you
Is as timeless as the universe
Brighter than the moon day sun
A long walk on a tropical beach
None of these things
Give me nearly the pleasure as
My love for you!

2012

Luxembourg

It was a cold rainy night
As we entered a small
Café in the Capital City
Of Luxembourg
We had driven several hours
Following a visit with friends in Beda, Holland
Our romantic journey had taken us
From Paris, France through
Holland and Belgium
We were now headed to the south of France
To visit friends and the wine country
Of Bandol-Sanary, at the Golfe du Lion
The waiter directed
Us to the Hotel Parc Beaux Art
Several blocks walk from the café
To this day I get cold chills
When I recall us standing
Nude on the balcony of our room
On that very cold, rainy, moonlit night
Overlooking The Royal Palace in the Park
Behind this petite picturesque hotel
Thanks, Chateauneuf-du-pape

8/1/2010

Love: A Question

Yesterday we spoke of love
It was as if we were blessed from above
We hugged and kissed
We made time-stopping love
Bonding our undying love
Today I awoke at dawn
To find you gone!
I am perplexed
As you must know
Wondering, why you had to go?
We spoke for hours of a future together
You must have thought of us apart
Now I lie here alone
With a broken heart

2002

Love Is Love

I always hear people say, "I lost my love."
I am not sure what that means.
For me love can never be lost. "Love is love!"
It is there whether or not you want it.
Love neither comes nor goes.
Love does not ebb or flow.
Love is there even if you can't see it or touch it.
Love is not there through thick and thin.
For love there is no beginning or end!
Love is not around the corner or 'round the bend.
You are not in love or out of love!
Love doesn't come from below or from above.
You didn't love and lose.
Love doesn't make you happy or give you the blues.
You neither gave love nor received love!
Love is not something you can give or take.
Love is there whether you are asleep or awake.
We are making love an empty word.
When we say, "I love, he loves, she loves.
I am in love, I am not in love, and I love candy,
I love cake!" Love, love, love for goodness' sake!
Love seems to be the beginning or end
of almost every sentence we speak!
Love is something we all appear to seek.
We don't know what it is, so why is it so important!
Love is the most overused, misused, and most misunderstood word
in almost every language of this world!
I would not begin to suggest you not use the word "love,"
for I can't seem to find a better word to describe my feelings
or to give real meaning to the words I use for someone I truly do
love! However, as a poet I am concerned that we owe

each other and the world a duty to use the word love
as it was always meant to be used—
to express to another (person) what we really feel when we love!
That we give all we have in love. Not for what
we expect to receive for such gifts from above!
God gives us each the power and ability to love!
Love is love—nothing more, nothing less!
It is by God's love, we are blessed!
I only request you stop and think the next time
you want to use this word, love!

Printed in the USA
CPSIA information can be obtained
at www.ICGtesting.com
LVHW091531050424
776545LV00002B/270